Halloweird: A book of morbid poems

Chelsey Silveira

BookLeaf Publishing

Presentation by *BookLeaf Publishing*

Web: www.bookleafpub.com

E-mail: info@bookleafpub.com

ISBN: 9789357447386

First edition 2022

DEDICATION

To the person who ignited my love of all things spooky or all together ookie, Sherry G. Silveira.

Wild Man

They call me Sasquatch, which is Salish for
"wild man."
I've wandered these lands since it all began.

I dwell in the forest in near total isolation,
But don't feel bad for me, as I prefer the
separation.

They study my legend in a pseudoscience called
Cryptozoology,
They also say these are the type of people in
need of psychology.

But do not be mistaken,
As I really hate getting my picture taken.

It could be all this matted hair, my flat nose or
awkward gait,
But if I'm being totally honest, I've gained a little
weight.

You would think being 15 feet tall would give
me better proportions,
But I digress, I must start counting my blessings,
not my misfortunes.

I guess I would have to say the best part about
being me
Is not about being famous or fuzzy clips shown
of me on TV

It's about the freedom of knowing absolutely no
stress,
I own no possessions, yet feel like I live in
excess

Being surrounded by nature and breathing air
that is fresh and pure,
I wouldn't give any of this up, so I'll probably
forever stay obscure.

Because even I think your society is kinda
freaky,
Sorry if saying so makes me sound a little
cheeky.

So, this is why whenever you happen to see me,
I instantly flee
Because us wild men want to stay wild and
forever fancy-free.

The Saddening, Maddening Legend of La Llorona

The wailing shrieks of La Llorona dressed all in
white
Shrill, full of hopelessness and despair
Her shame and pain consume the night.

She drown her children after discovering her
husband's affair
The realization of what she had done drove her
to suicide
She drown herself too, thinking she had ended
her nightmare.

But unbeknownst to her, there were spiritual
rules to abide,
She was doomed to search for her children in a
purgatory that will never end
An otherworldly punishment surely worse than
being crucified.

La Llorona will forever go beyond the limits of
those who transcend,
Searching for and collecting souls for penance.
Doing whatever morbid deeds she can to amend.

The Witches Domain

Dancing on your graves
There is no day like Samhain.
Cauldron bubbling and boiling
The flesh off the bones of the slain.

Black magic, the occult and the summoning of
spirits
The evil within our cold hearts knows no bounds
or earthly limits.

Seeking power through divination
Opening up Pandora's Box.
We will be the cause of total annihilation,
Just you watch.

Dancing on your graves
There is no day like Samhain.
Your mortal coil unraveling
This astral plane is now the witches domain.

Withering Wendigo

An insatiable hunger that can never be
suppressed.
Decaying flesh draped over moss covered bones,
Beware false idols made of stones.
Wendigo has an appetite that will forever be at
unrest.

The smell of blood, sweat and tears, it is
obsessed.
Cannibalistic greed breeds clones,
An undead army of drones.
There are so many souls that have been
possessed.

Grim

Shrouded in darkness, scythe in hand,
Grim Reaper comes to collect you.
Walking side-by-side through oblivion, just you
two.
He deciphers the entirety of your life, so that
you understand.

Life is what you make it, the wheels of fate do
not control.
He shows you it's not about the harvest you reap,
but the seeds you sow.
Like the tides of time, everything has its ebb and
flow.
You are now ready and willing to hand over your
soul.

Dying for Dracula

He said he has crossed oceans of time to find
me.
His lust pumping like the blood through my
veins.

An eternal embrace to bind thee,
The crimson drips and stains.

My heart and spirit engulfed in flames,
The light within me dims
Every fibre of my being encased in chains.

The red hot burning inside me brims
To the surface of my mind
Please forgive me of my sins.

His body and mine forever intertwined,
My afterlife begins.

Beware The Bogeyman

The Bogeyman haunts those who misbehave
Sleepless nightmares fill the night
Your flavour of fear he will always crave

He lurks in the shadows out of the light
He hides in your closet and under your bed
Try all you might to keep The Bogeyman out of
mind and out of sight

But there is nothing you can do to get him out of
your head
He will swallow you up entirely with petrified
fright
Slowly devouring your soul until you wish you
were dead.

Dominion of Demons

Demons depend on depravity
Devout in deep depression
Devious in displaying duality
Distinguished in deflection

Diabolical by discreet domination
Debauchery through daunting detentions
Dedication in drumming up devastation
Delighted by dangerous dissensions

Demons depend on dissimilarity
Devout in deep digression
Devious in displaying dimensionality
Distinguished in deception

Vampyr

Dancing with a succubus,
Surrounded by glowing flames.
Succumbing to the black abyss,
The fire within me she claims.

Haiku #1: Chupacabra

Oh, Chupacabra
Stinking goat sucking mongrel
Mystic dog creature.

Haiku #2: Gremlin

Gremlin in the air
Wrecking and crashing the plane
No one believes me

Haiku #3: Kraken

Release the Kraken
Tentacles rise overhead
Shipwrecked and all wet

Haiku #4: Cyclops

One big eye to see
What is that in front of me?
Cyclops is clumsy

Haiku #5: Leprechaun

Pot of gold treasure
At the end of a rainbow
Looting Leprechauns

Haiku #6: Demon Eyes

Demon eyes glowing
Searing deep into my soul
Possession begins

Creature Feature

Creature of the night
What a formidable sight

Creature of the night
Fill me with your black light

Creature of the night
What a soul sucking bite

Creature of the night
Fill me with unimaginable fright

Creature of the night
What is left of me that is able to fight?

Creature of the night
Fill me with all your plight

Brundle Fly

Against all logical convention,
He created an unbelievable invention,
That dealt in the realm teleportation.

Without hesitation,
Or a thought of self preservation,
He used himself as experimentation.

He did every minute calculation,
Entered his 'telepod' contraption,
But unbeknownst to him there was a
cross-contamination.

A common house fly was accidentally added to
the equation,
That resulted in a crude amalgamation,
A distrurbing DNA mutation.

During his morbidly painful degeneration,
He had to feed through the process of acidic
regurgitation,
His flesh rotting away in slow decomposition.

In his final transformation,
He caused almost total and utter annihilation,

But through all the turmoil and devastation,

He was able to make the distinction,
That would be his last dying salvation,
To save the woman he loved beyond devotion.

Because before his execution,
They entwined in carnal copulation,
That resulted in a human-fly hybrid evolution.

By that through his son's extension,
He was able to have a sort of redemption,
By successfully curing this monstrous hereditary
affliction.

Devil's Pie

The devil's pie
Is a slice of lies.

But you can't deny
Those demonic eyes.

The devil's sly
In any disguise.

There is no need to question why
Your own demise.

The devil's high
From your hopeless cries.

The end is nigh
Cut all your ties.

The devil's pie
Tastes bittersweet as your soul dies.

This is the devil's design